Twenty-One Elephants
AND STILL STANDING

Written by **APRIL JONES PRINCE** Illustrated by **FRANÇOIS ROCA**

HOUGHTON MIFFLIN COMPANY BOSTON 2005

For fourteen years, they'd watched it rise—
the cities' schoolteachers, bankers,
cabinetmakers,
pointing and gawking, ooohing and aaahing,
cheering as the great pillars grew.
Then came woven steel cables,
strung graceful and strong,
like stairways straight to the stars.

Taller and longer, bigger and broader,
a bridge of infinite dreams.
New York and Brooklyn, dwarfed by its arches,
knew the future had entered their sights.
Amazing, worth the waiting,
it was simply breathtaking.
The Eighth Wonder of the World.

Some wondered how long it would stand.

When the day finally came
and the Brooklyn Bridge opened
the landmark was given its due:
flags waved, bands played, kids hoorayed
before bigwigs in top hats galore.
At night there were fireworks, skyrockets of light
that rained for an hour
from the top of the towers
to the roar of the crowds down below.
Packed on sailboats and steamers,
amidst bright-colored streamers,
people partied until the sun rose.

For the two sister cities,
there was special excitement;
they were linked by a magnificent bond.
Now over the river, not on its swift current,
they could visit, do business, see sights.
Sweethearts could take moonlit strolls.

The bridge was exquisite, a true work of art.
The greatest feat of its day.
But so long and so lofty, its cables so new—
some had to ask,
Is it safe?

To these doubt-ridden few

friends sang the thing's virtues:

"The arches!"

"The trusswork!"

"The VIEW!"

Still . . .

Some could not be persuaded:

"Similar bridges have fallen!

Who wants to bargain

this bridge won't dance in the wind?"

One man who heard this, Phineas T. Barnum,
saw in the doubt an opportunity.
For Phineas T. Barnum
always looked on the bright side.
Phineas T. Barnum was larger than life.
The world-famous showman's
most awesome creation?
"The Greatest Show on Earth."

Yet Barnum's ideas weren't contained
by a tent.
"I will stage an event
that will calm every fear, erase every worry,
about that remarkable bridge.
My display will amuse, inform,
and astound.
Or else my name isn't Barnum!"

So one evening in May 1884,
the circus headed for Brooklyn.
It traveled by water
except for old Barnum's
most massive, most gallant attractions.

Up Broadway they sauntered,
trainers and charges,
enchanting more than a few.
Onlookers went wild
and filed behind,
beguiled by the pachyderm procession.
For the public prized elephants,
especially Jumbo, pride of the circus's rings.
With his height of twelve feet,
the good-natured beast
was America's oversize darling.

On the group marched,
past City Hall,
past mothers, fathers, and children.
Then the bridge, straight ahead!
The spectacle mounting
with the giants' first steps on the roadway.

One after another,

the elephants pressed onward,

silently trusting the wood planks and steel.

Five, six, then seven were crossing.

Ten, eleven—and still there were more!

Some onlookers ogled; some giggled with glee.

Some questioned companions or strangers:

How many pounds

can the wondrous bridge hold?

How many elephants are too great a load?

Swaying and rumbling, still they were coming,

the parade of elephant bulk.

At the end of the line came Jumbo himself,
for twenty-one elephants in all.
The seven-ton star
seemed to waggle his ears
in reply to admirers' cheers.

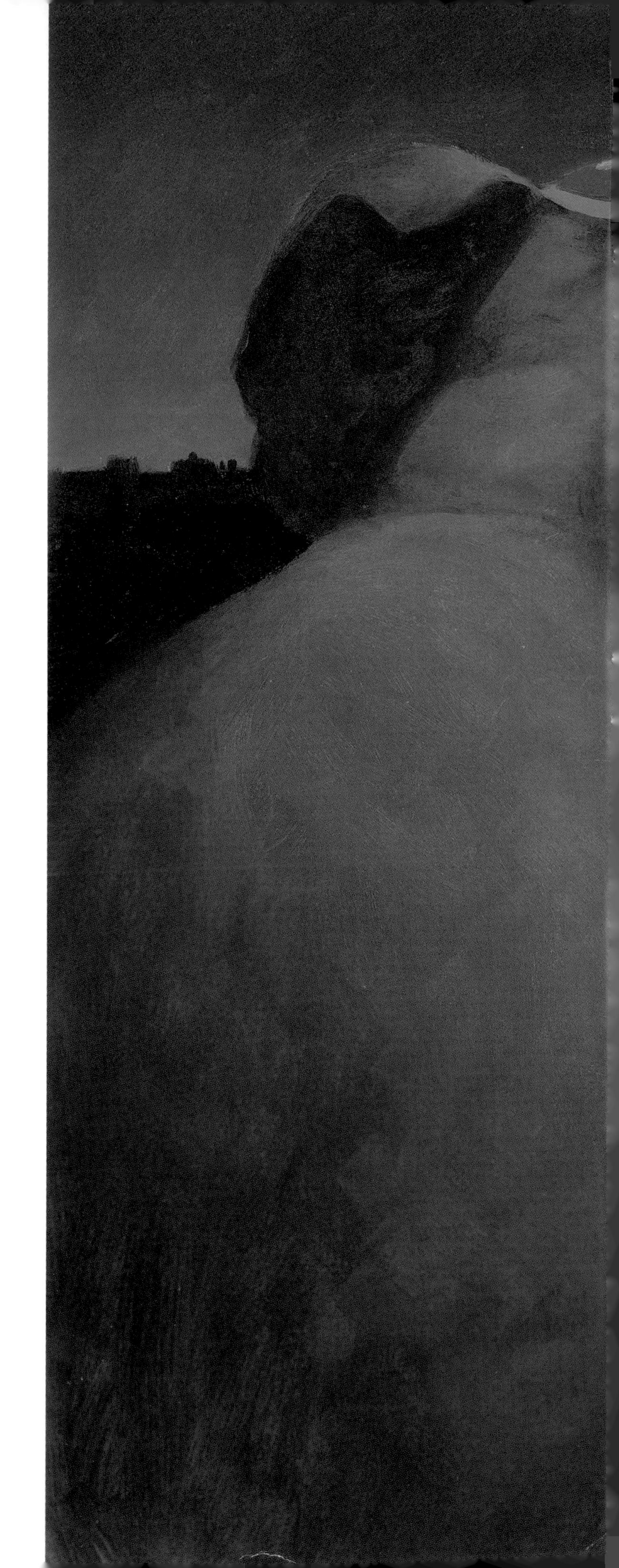

NEW YORK BROOKLYN

And though the bridge stretched a mile,
in just a short while—
and much to the people's delight—
the elephants had crossed,
with the bridge still aloft.
Barnum pronounced the thing sound.

In the following days,
some doubters strolled
the greatest bridge on earth.
What else did they do,
once they'd savored the view?

RIHMOND & STOVE CO

Why, they went to the Big Top, of course!

— Author's Note —

When I first learned of the event described in this book, I could hardly believe it was true. Had P. T. Barnum really trusted the extraordinary, but also newly completed, Brooklyn Bridge with some of his most valuable and beloved attractions? Determined to find out everything I could, I traveled to museums and libraries, scrolled through old newspapers, viewed documentaries, scoured books old and new, and called upon experts.

I learned a great deal—including the fact that I could not learn it all. Because of gaps in the historical record, I couldn't determine, for example, whether Barnum crossed the bridge with his elephants that night, or whether he met them in Brooklyn. In the end, I chose to include him in the crossing because he was certainly there in spirit: the idea was his, the elephants were his, and the stunt accomplished his goals of causing a stir and linking his name with that of the magnificent bridge.

For all the pieces of the puzzle I couldn't solve, I turned up a wealth of other information that helped me understand the elephants' crossing. I discovered that elephants have been used to demonstrate the strength of bridges not only because of the animals' great weight—each weighs about 10,000 pounds—but also because they are known to test surfaces with their trunks or front feet to keep from crossing unsafe structures. I found that P. T. Barnum was a pioneer of modern advertising and popular entertainment; he was world-famous for his wild curiosities and amusements, and for his even wilder promotion of them. I learned about the can-do spirit of the late nineteenth century, about bridges and bridge building, and about the remarkable Roebling family, who designed and built the Brooklyn Bridge. If you are interested in any of these topics, you might enjoy these books and Web sites:

Curlee, Lynn. *Brooklyn Bridge*. New York: Atheneum, 2001.
Mann, Elizabeth. *The Brooklyn Bridge*. New York: Mikaya Press, 1996.
Redmond, Ian. *Elephant*. New York: Dorling Kindersley, 2000.
Worth, Bonnie. *Jumbo: The Most Famous Elephant in the World*. New York: Random House, 2001.
www.barnum-museum.org
www.americaslibrary.gov/cgi-bin/page.cgi/jb/nation/barnum_1
www.americaslibrary.gov/cgi-bin/page.cgi/jb/nation/bbridge_1

For my family—David, Charlie, Mom, Dad, Chip, Nan, Dick, Karen, Susan, and Gram—with love and gratitude for supporting me and my work. —A.J.P.

To Charlotte, Suzanne, and Angèle. —F.R.

For their generous assistance the author would like to thank Susan Aprill, archivist of the Brooklyn Collection at the Brooklyn Public Library; Kathleen Maher, curator of the Barnum Museum; Joseph Mahoney, supervisor of mammals for the Wildlife Conservation Society at the Bronx Zoo; Melanie Bower, collections access assistant at the Museum of the City of New York; and Mary Witkowski, city historian of the Historical Collection at the Bridgeport Public Library.

---

www.houghtonmifflinbooks.com

Library of Congress Cataloging-in-Publication Data
Prince, April Jones.
Twenty-one elephants and still standing : a story of P.T. Barnum and the Brooklyn Bridge / by April Jones Prince ; illustrated by François Roca.
p. cm.
Summary: Upon completion of the Brooklyn Bridge, P.T. Barnum and his twenty-one elephants parade across to prove to everyone that the bridge is safe.
ISBN 0-618-44887-X
1. Brooklyn Bridge (New York, N.Y.)—History—Juvenile fiction. 2. Barnum, P. T. (Phineas Taylor), 1810-1891—Juvenile fiction. [1. Brooklyn Bridge (New York, N.Y.)—History—Fiction. 2. Barnum, P.T. (Phineas Taylor), 1810-1891—Fiction. 3. Jumbo (Elephant)—Fiction. 4. Elephants—Fiction.] I. Roca, François, ill. II. Title.
PZ7.P93585Tw 2005 [E]—dc22 2004005229

ISBN-13: 978-0618-44887-6

Printed in Singapore TWP 10 9 8 7 6 5 4 3 2 1